Living in Space

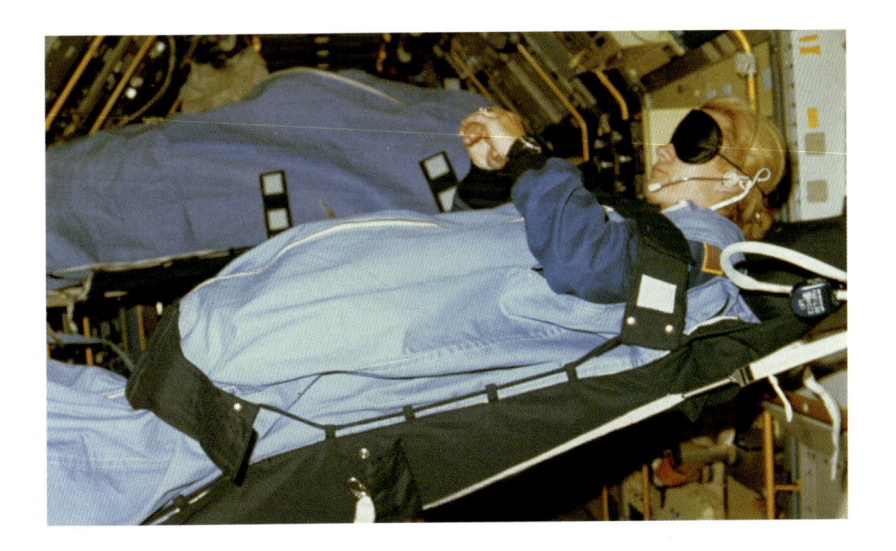

Robyn Opie

ETA Cuisenaire

ETA Cuisenaire
800-445-5985   www.etacuisenaire.com

Living in Space

ISBN 0-7406-2793-7
ETA 305071

ETA/Cuisenaire • Vernon Hills, IL 60061-1862
800-445-5985 • www.etacuisenaire.com

Published by ETA/Cuisenaire® under license from Reed International Pty Ltd
All rights reserved.

Text © 2001 Robyn Opie
Designer: Andrea Jaretzki
Acknowledgments: Cover, Page 3, Digital Vision; all other images, NASA.

No part of this publication may be reproduced, stored in a retrieval system, or transmitted, in any form or by any means, electronic, mechanical, photocopying, recording, or otherwise, without the prior written permission of the publisher.

Printed by SNP SPrint Pte Ltd Singapore

03 04 05 06 07 08 09 10 11 12   10 9 8 7 6 5 4 3 2 1

Living in Space

Astronauts work in space. When they work in space, they live in a spacecraft. A spacecraft is kind of like a floating house. It has all the things the astronauts need to live in space. What is it like for astronauts living in space? Here are some questions and answers to help you find out.

When a spacecraft takes off, everything the astronauts will need is on board.

Why do astronauts float around in space?

In space, things are weightless. Astronauts in space float around because they are weightless. On Earth, things aren't weightless. An invisible force called gravity pulls things toward the ground.

This astronaut could be standing on the ceiling!

Feeling Sick in Space

Sometimes all that floating around in space makes astronauts feel "space sick." Space sickness is a bit like sea sickness.

There is no right-side up in space.

How do astronauts breathe in space?

A spacecraft must supply air for the astronauts. There is no air in space, so a spacecraft gives them air to breathe.

How do astronauts get water to drink?

A spacecraft must supply water for the astronauts. There is no water in space. Water is brought from Earth. Enough water must be brought for the entire crew for the whole journey. The water is usually stored in big bags.

water bag

How do astronauts take showers?

Astronauts can't take showers on a spacecraft, but they do have ways to keep themselves clean. Astronauts get water from a machine that has warm and cold water. Astronauts use two washcloths. They use one washcloth to put on liquid soap. They use the other washcloth to remove the soap.

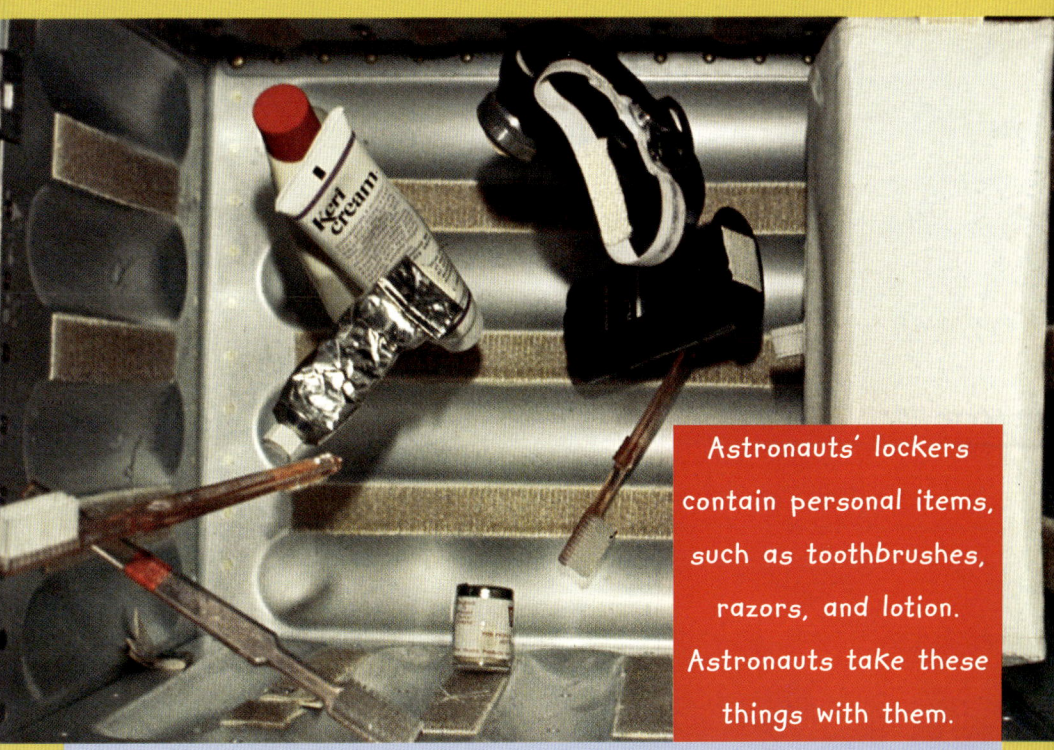

Astronauts' lockers contain personal items, such as toothbrushes, razors, and lotion. Astronauts take these things with them.

Did You Know?
On Earth, people use about 12 gallons of water every time they take a shower. Astronauts wash themselves with less than 1 gallon of water.

How do astronauts brush their teeth?

Astronauts brush their teeth like we do on Earth. Astronauts wet their toothbrush with a cloth, since there are no faucets. They clean the toothbrush with a wet cloth. There is no sink, so an astronaut spits out the toothpaste into a tissue.

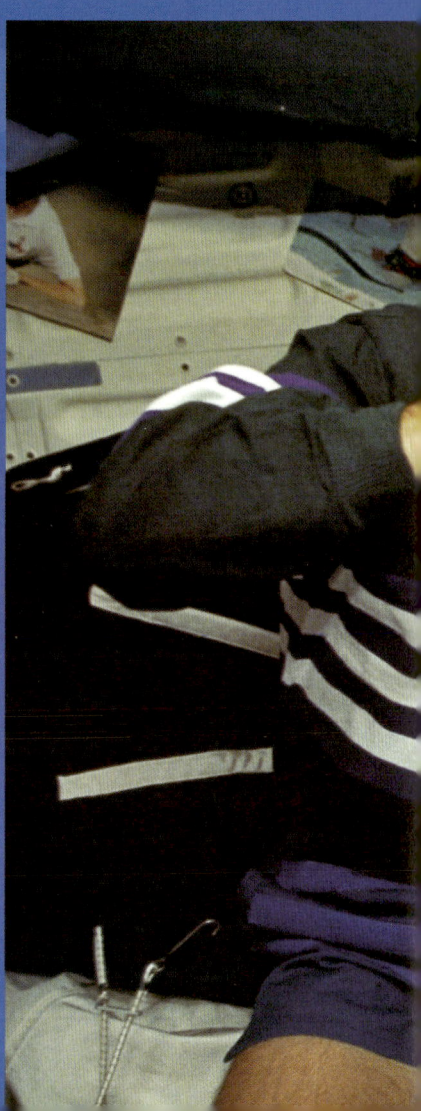

How do astronauts wash their hair?

Astronauts use damp washcloths to wash their hair. They use a special shampoo. They wipe the shampoo through their hair with a damp washcloth. Then they use another damp washcloth to wipe out the shampoo.

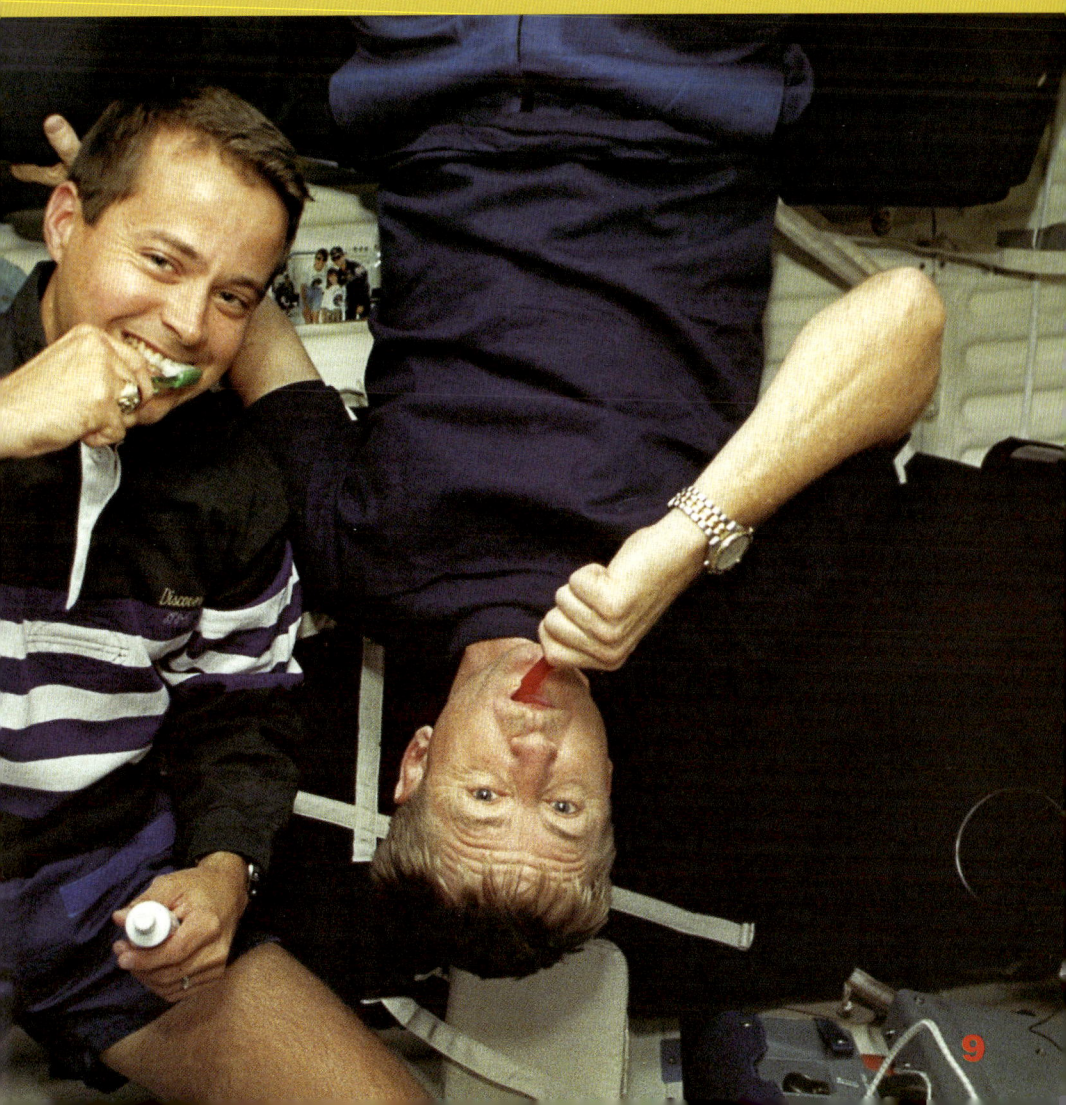

How do astronauts go to the bathroom?

There are toilets on a spacecraft. A spacecraft toilet works a little bit like an airplane toilet. A stream of air carries the waste away. Solid waste is stored in containers. The containers are removed when the spacecraft returns to Earth. Urine goes out into space.

Hold On!

A spacecraft toilet has foot straps. These stop the astronaut from floating away!

This is the type of toilet that is used on a spacecraft.

How do astronauts wash their clothes?

Astronauts don't have to wash their clothes! There are no washing machines or dryers on a spacecraft. Astronauts put their dirty clothes in airtight plastic bags. The dirty clothes are kept in the bags until the spacecraft returns to Earth.

These astronauts are putting a storage bag into place.

What does an astronaut eat?

Astronauts do eat some fresh food, such as tortillas, bread, fruit, and cookies. They mostly eat pre-cooked meals, which are brought with them on board. The pre-cooked meals are in packets that are heated before they're eaten. They are sort of like the meals you can buy in supermarkets.

This meal has food in packets and a drink in a can.

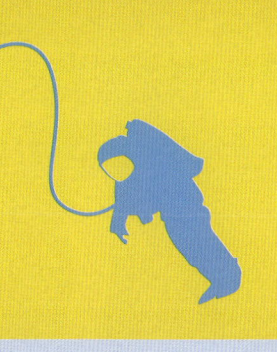

Space Menu

Find out what an astronaut might eat in a day. Make a menu for breakfast, lunch, and dinner.

Did You Know?

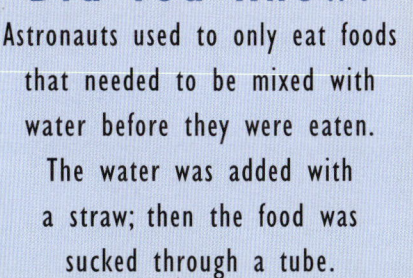

Astronauts used to only eat foods that needed to be mixed with water before they were eaten. The water was added with a straw; then the food was sucked through a tube.

This astronaut is adding water to a packet of food. The water comes from a special machine.

13

How do astronauts eat?

Meal times are a bit strange on a spacecraft. Food is served on a tray. The tray is kind of like a plate, but it can be attached to something. If not, dinner would float away! The tray can be attached to the astronaut's lap. If the astronaut wants to stand and eat, the food tray can be strapped to the wall.

The food tray is divided into sections to hold the different kinds of food. Each kind of food is in a packet. The food packets have strips that stick to the tray so they don't float away.

Notice the foot straps that the astronaut needs while she eats.

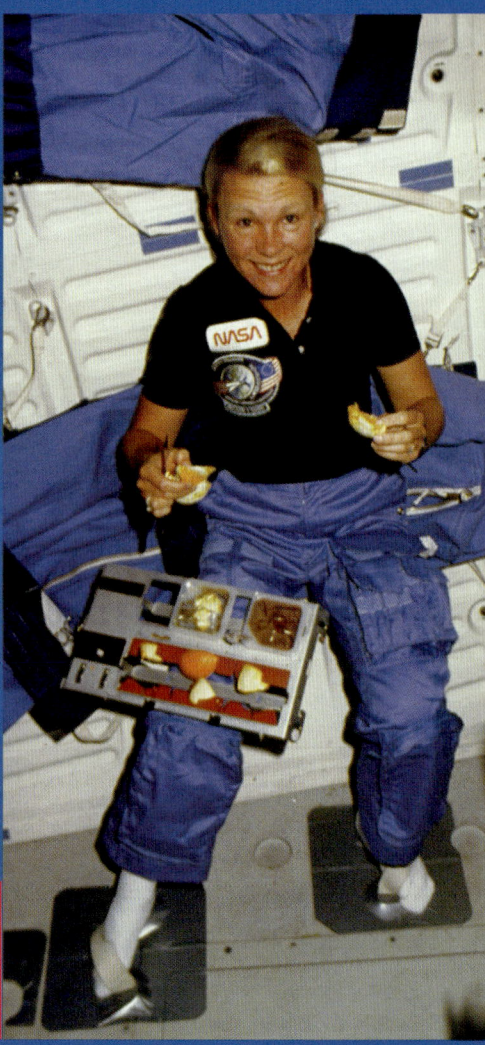

An astronaut uses a knife, a fork, and a spoon. An astronaut needs a pair of scissors at mealtime, too. The scissors are for opening the packets of food!

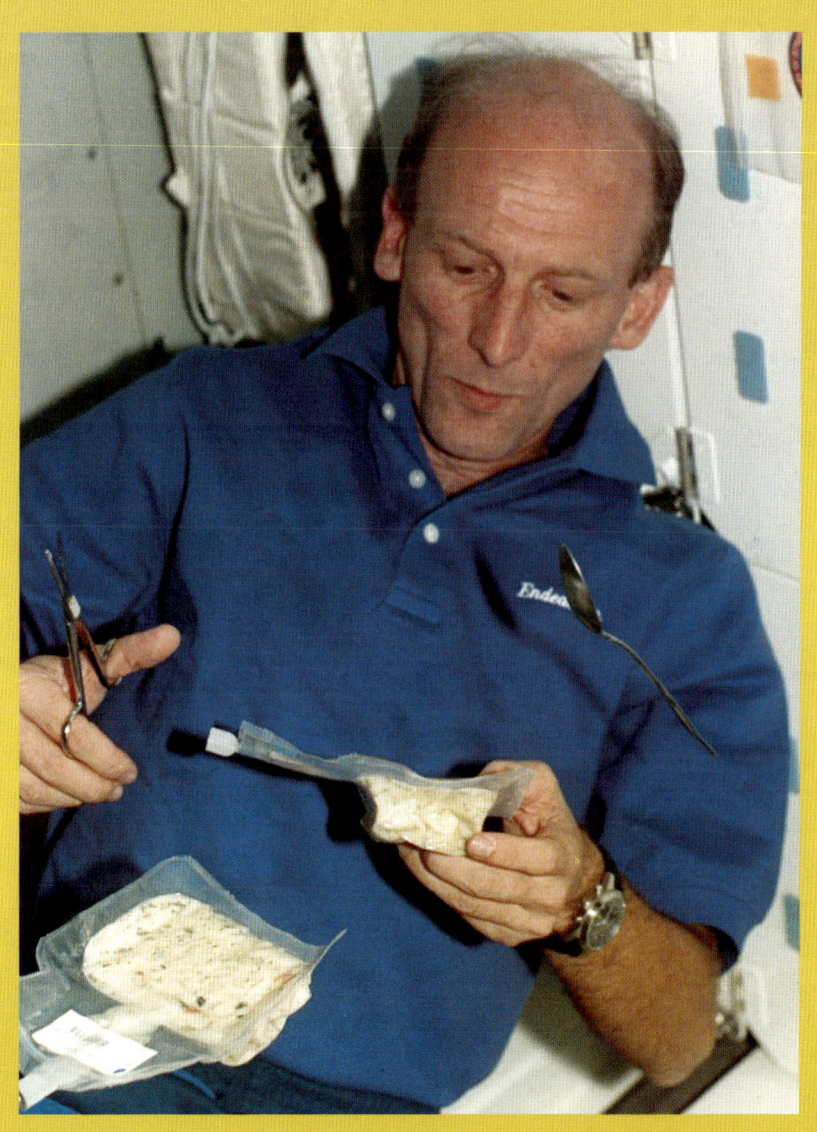

Danger! Crumbs on the Loose

Astronauts need to be careful when they are eating and drinking. Crumbs and drops of juice can float in the air. If crumbs or juice are on the loose, they can damage the expensive equipment on board.

There is an energy drink in the packet with the straw. The astronaut will drink it before he goes on a space walk.

Did You Know?

Astronauts can't shake salt onto their fries. Spacecraft salt is mixed with water and pepper is mixed with oil. Astronauts have to mix the wet salt and oily pepper into their meals. That way, an astronaut can add salt and pepper to a meal without the little grains of salt and pepper floating away.

These bags of snack food are stuck to Velcro. Why?

Do astronauts wash the dishes?

Astronauts do not wash the dishes because there is not enough water on a spacecraft. When the astronauts have finished their meals, everything is cleaned with damp cloths. Scraps are put into containers and stored.

Some trash is put into airtight bags like this.

This astronaut is pushing the trash bags into a storage container. The trash will be removed once the spacecraft has landed back on Earth.

Where do astronauts sleep?

Astronauts sleep in special sleeping bags. Some of the crew sleep on bunk beds. Astronauts don't have to lie down to sleep because they're weightless. Some astronauts strap their sleeping bags to the wall of the shuttle and sleep standing up. When you're weightless, sleeping strapped to a wall is comfortable!

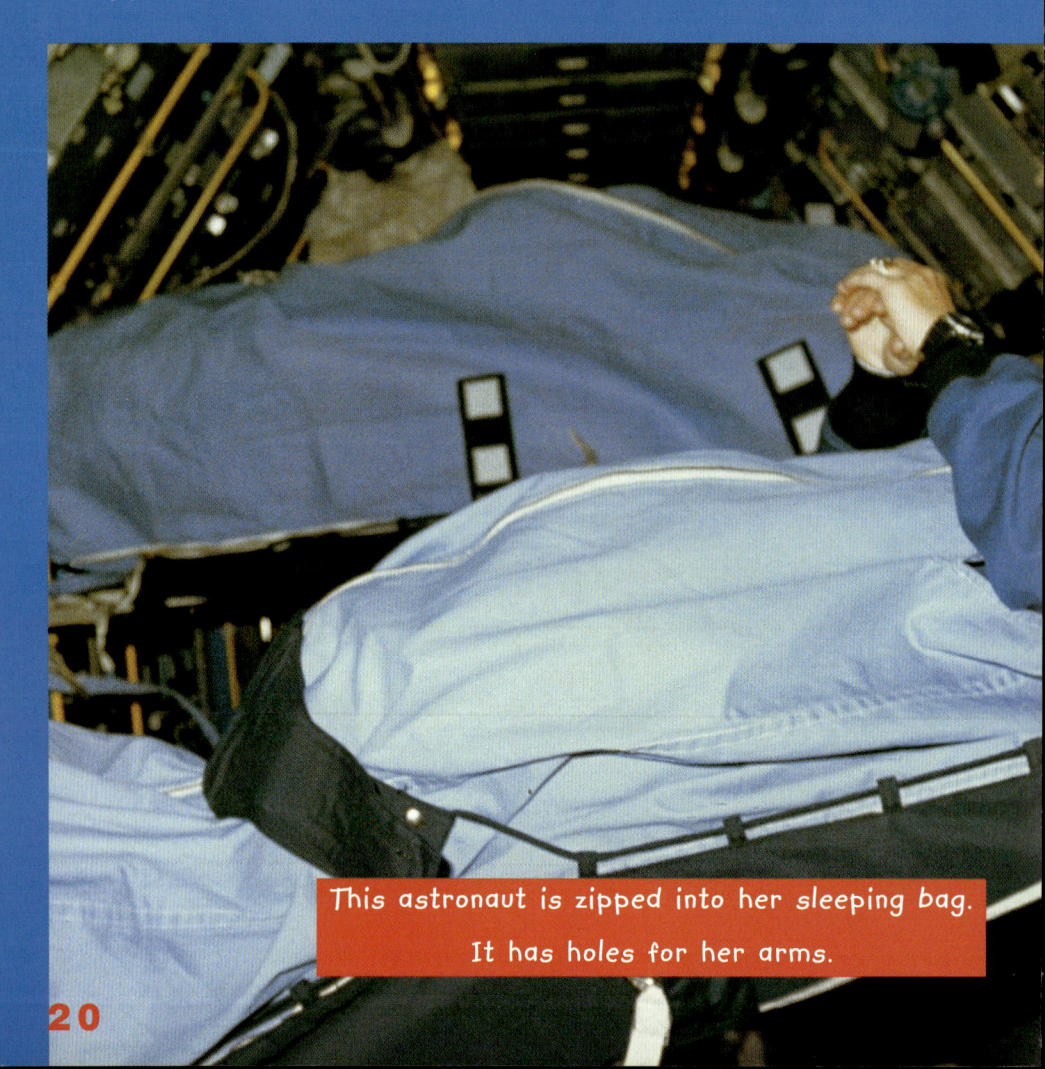

This astronaut is zipped into her sleeping bag. It has holes for her arms.

Bunk Beds in Space

Spacecraft bunk beds are padded boards with sleeping bags attached to them. The beds would feel hard on Earth, but they feel soft in space.

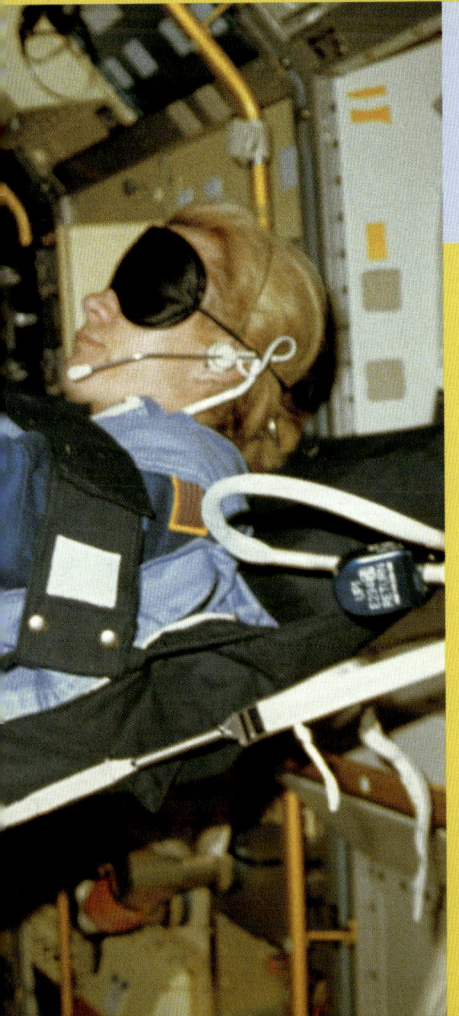

Did You Know?
All astronauts have to be strapped down to sleep. Otherwise, they would float around the cabin. The straps go around the astronaut's arms and legs.

Sleeping Blindfolded

Day and night is different on a spacecraft. When astronauts are sleeping, they need to wear eye shades or blindfolds to help block out any light.

Why would an astronaut wear ear plugs?

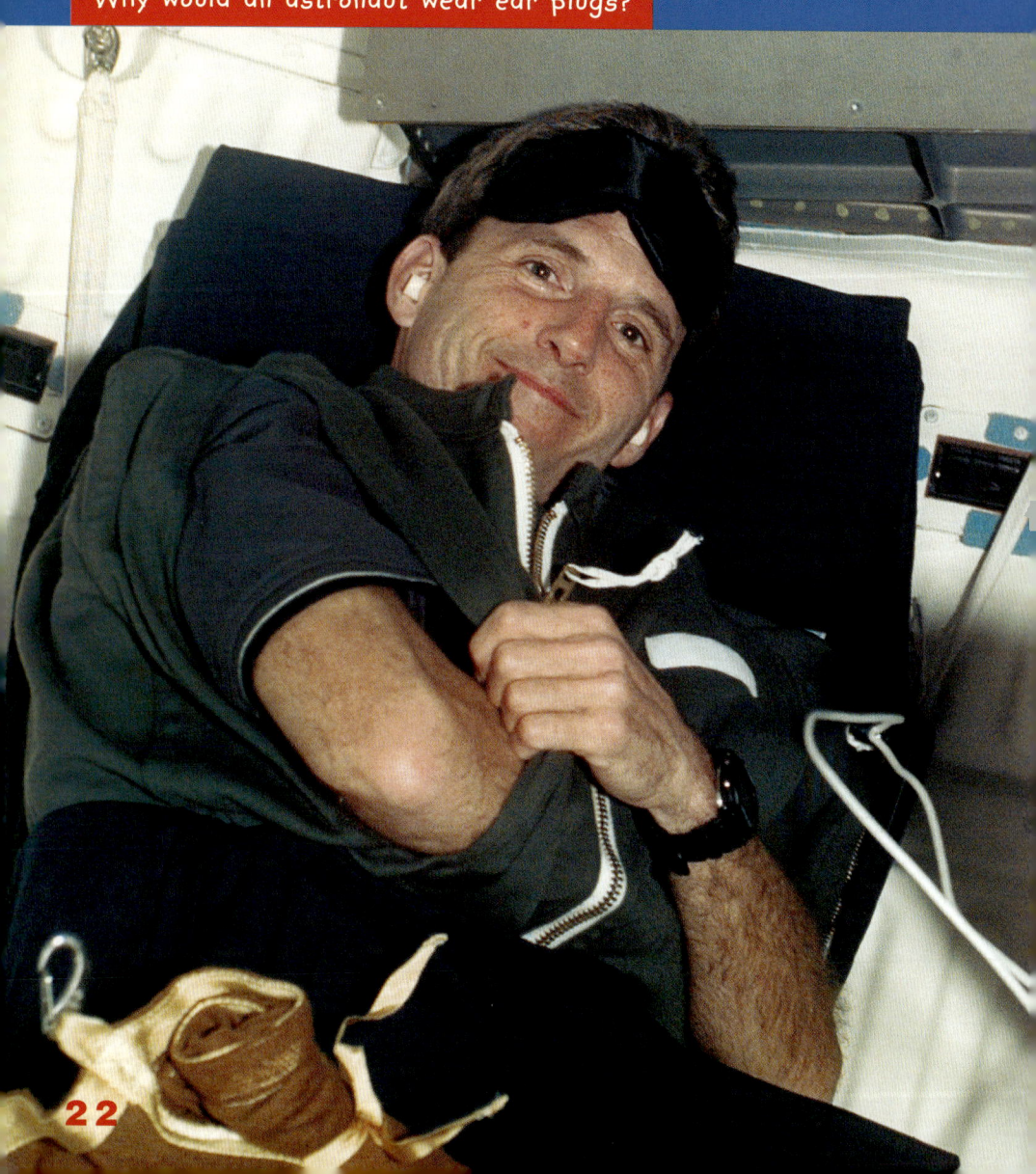

Some spacecraft have sleeping compartments. These have a light for reading. The compartments can also be closed so the astronaut has some privacy.

Did You Know?
Astronauts sleep for about the same amount of time in a spacecraft as they would on Earth.

Who is watching over the astronauts?

The astronauts are being watched over by Mission Control. Mission Control is the group of people on Earth that is supervising the spacecraft's flight. Even when the whole crew is sleeping, two astronauts usually wear headsets. That way, Mission Control can send an urgent message, if necessary.

Astronauts wear headsets. This is how they communicate with Mission Control.

Did You Know?
Mission Control can wake up astronauts with alarms!

This woman works at Mission Control in Houston.

What do astronauts wear to work?

When astronauts go outside the spacecraft, they have to wear space suits. A space suit has two parts, sort of like a shirt and pants. The pieces of a space suit snap together snugly. A space suit protects the astronaut's body from the heat and cold of outer space.

Space suits have a backpack. The backpack supplies air for the astronaut to breathe. An astronaut wears a helmet and gloves for protection, too. Without a space suit, the astronaut would die.

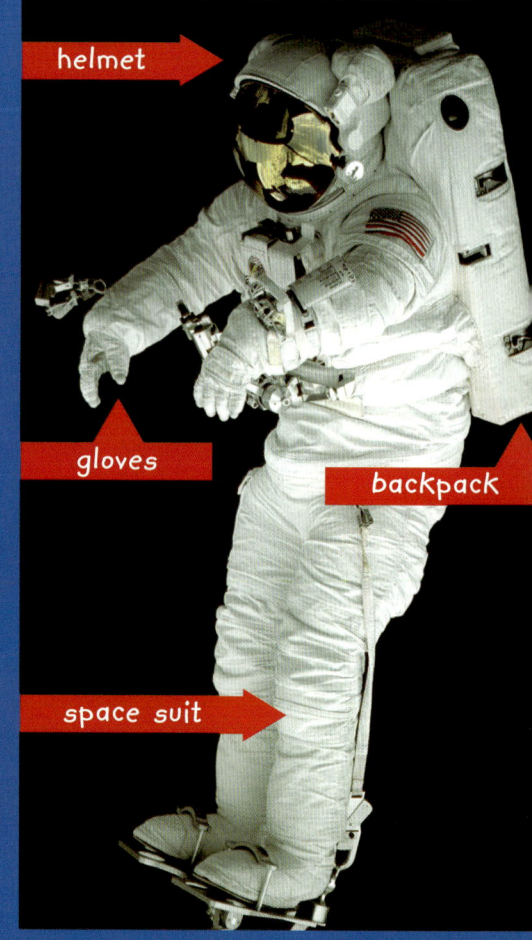

Did You Know?

Astronauts must carry a radio when they are outside the spacecraft. They use this to talk to the astronauts inside the spacecraft and to Mission Control.

This is what astronauts wear under their space suits.

How do astronauts exercise in space?

Astronauts use exercise bikes and treadmills to exercise in space. Astronauts' muscles and bones get weaker in space because they are not using them. To stay healthy, astronauts must exercise for 15 to 30 minutes each day.

This astronaut is on an exercise bike.

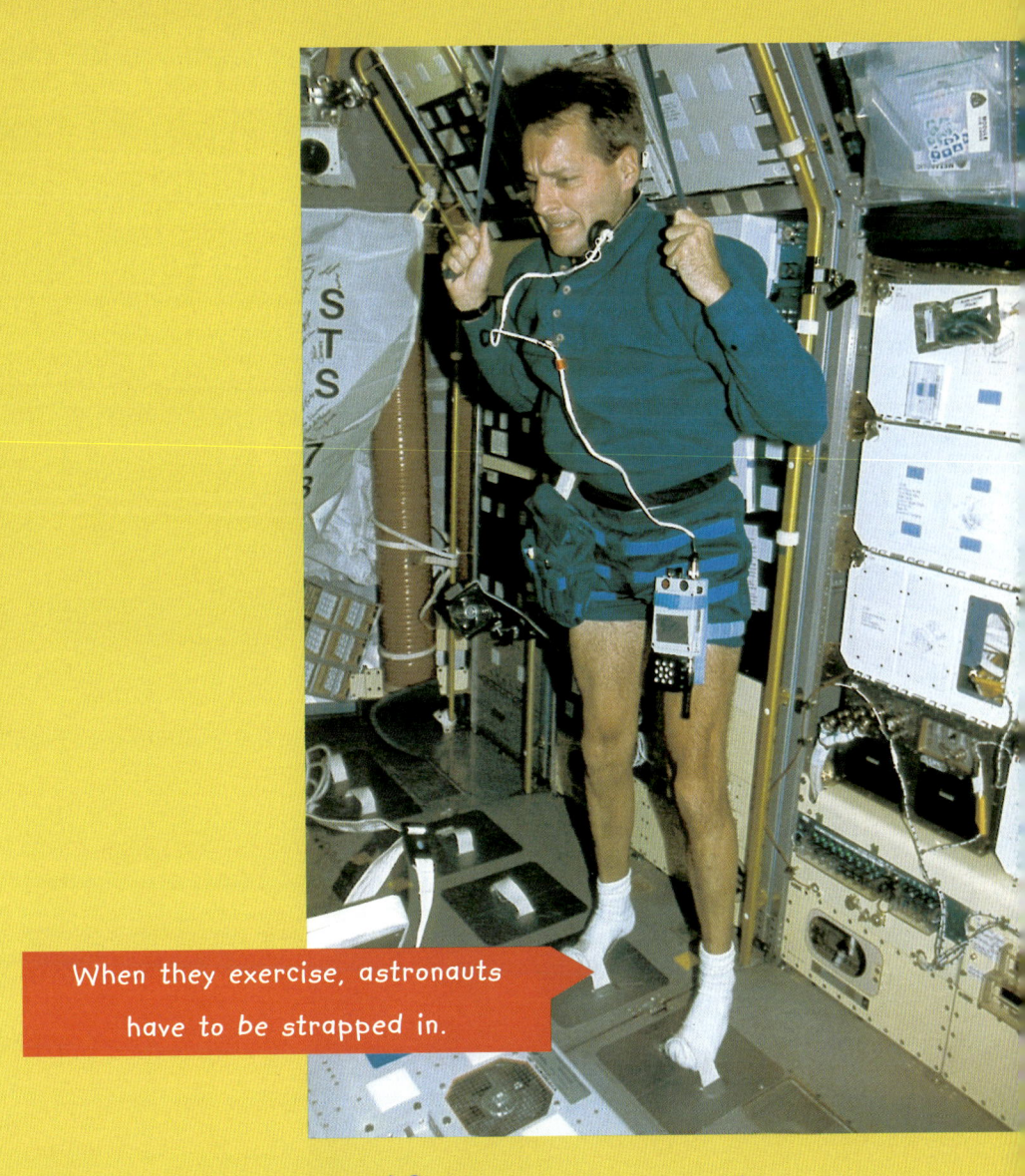

When they exercise, astronauts have to be strapped in.

What happens if an astronaut needs a doctor?

A spacecraft carries a medical kit. There is always one person on board who is especially trained to give medical care.

What do astronauts do for fun?

Astronauts take things like books, games, and music for their free time on board. Some astronauts like to take cameras with them and record what they see. Looking out the window is a favorite activity for astronauts, too!

Visit the NASA website to find out more about what it's like living in space.
http://www.nasa.gov/

This astronaut is taking photographs in his free time.

Glossary

airtight   no air can get in or out

compartment   one of the spaces that something is divided into

headset   earphones that fit on the head, used for sending and receiving messages

medical kit   bag or container that has useful medical supplies

spacecraft   vehicle for traveling in space

treadmill   an exercise machine that moves around when people tread or step on it

Index

backpack	26
blindfolds	22
bunk beds	20, 21
exercise	28, 29
eye shades	22
food	12, 13, 14, 15
gravity	4
headsets	24
medical kit	29
Mission Control	24, 25, 27
trash	19
scissors	15
showers	7
sleep	20, 21
sleeping bags	20
sleeping compartments	23
space suits	26, 27
spacecraft	3, 5, 6, 7, 10, 11, 14, 18, 19, 22, 23, 24, 26, 27
toilets	10
washcloths	7, 9
water	6, 7, 13, 18
weightless	4, 20